I·M·A·G·E·S

I·M·A·G·E·S

I·M·A·G·E·S

CONTEMPORARY CANADIAN REALISM

LESTER &ORPEN DENNYS PUBLISHERS

SELECTED BY MARCI LIPMAN AND LOUISE LIPMAN

Acknowledgements
Many people have made this book possible. In particular we would like to thank the artists and their families; Aggregation Gallery; Art Gallery of Winnipeg; Atelier Gallery; The Canada Council Art Bank; DeVooght Gallery; Dominion Gallery; Galerie Bernard Desroches; Gallery Moos; Hett Gallery; McIntosh Gallery; Mendel Art Gallery; M. F. Feheley Arts Company Ltd.; The National Gallery of Canada: Susan Campbell and Peter Smith; Polysar Ltd. Art Collection; Roberts Gallery; University of Western Ontario; Vie des Arts; Visual Arts Branch, Government of Alberta; Karyn Allen; Mr. and Mrs. Earl Green; and Leland and Anne Verner.

We gratefully acknowledge the assistance of the Canada Council Explorations Program.

Printed by Ashton Potter Limited

Colour co-ordination by M.P. Graphics Limited

Typesetting by Trigraph

Bound by Holmes Bindery Services Limited

Design by Paul Hodgson for Fifty Fingers

Production by Verbatim

Photo Credits:

Erik Dzenis, p. 13; John Evans, p. 19; Fischer Fine Art Ltd., London, p. 43; Courtesy of the Gallery Moos, Toronto, p. 29; Robert Keziere (Courtesy of the Atelier Gallery, Vancouver), p. 35; Les Krizan, p. 25; Ian MacEachern (Courtesy of the McIntosh Gallery, London), p. 33; Ernest Mayer, pp. 29, 41; Tom Moore, pp. 7, 9, 11, 15, 17, 21, 31, 37, 45; Regon and Associates (Courtesy of the Hett Gallery, Edmonton), p. 27; Ron Vickers, p. 23.

Canadian Cataloguing in Publication Data

Main entry under title:
Images

ISBN 0-919630-35-9

1. Painting, Canadian. 2. Painting, Modern—20th century—Canada. 3. Realism in art—Canada.
I. Lipman, Marci, 1948- II. Lipman, Louise, 1953-

ND245.I42   759.11   C80-09 4726-6

Printed and bound in Canada for
Lester & Orpen Dennys Limited
78 Sullivan Street
Toronto, Ontario M5T 1C1

Realism, as we refer to it in this book, means representational art—art in which the subjects are part of our everyday experience. There is a tendency to think that realist painters duplicate their surroundings; in fact, they borrow from them, adding to or deleting from their subjects, highlighting or varying form or colour to give us their highly personal interpretations of the things most familiar to us.

IMAGES includes varying styles of realism, from magic to high. The artists share a common commitment to accurate detail in the presentation of their subjects and to the meticulous and painstaking planning which forms the framework upon which the image is constructed. A single painting may often take several months to complete and the original idea may be refined in the process; the artist's original vision, however, is faithfully retained.

Realism is not a new art form—its roots in Canada go back to the nineteenth century. In IMAGES we have tried to represent each region of the country in order to give an overview of contemporary realism in Canada. As in our first book of Canadian art, TWENTY/TWENTY, our choice of paintings was of necessity limited by the format and several excellent artists had to be left out. Of those artists included, some are already well known in Canada as well as abroad; others do not as yet have firmly established reputations. Many of the paintings are brand new; none of them have ever before been reproduced in this format.

The intention and design of IMAGES is that each painting can be removed and framed for a personal collection. And, seen together, these twenty paintings clearly reflect in spirit and imagination the calibre of representational art in Canada.

Marci Lipman was born in Toronto and studied Fine Arts at York University. She is a leading art consultant and the owner of Marci Lipman Graphics in Toronto—Canada's major fine-art poster house. Louise Lipman studied at Bard College and the University of British Columbia. She is a publisher of fine-art posters and the owner of Lipman Publishing Inc.

IMAGES

1

Mary Pratt
''Tied Boat''
Oil on board, 18″ x 18″, 1980
Courtesy of the Aggregation Gallery, Toronto
Private collection

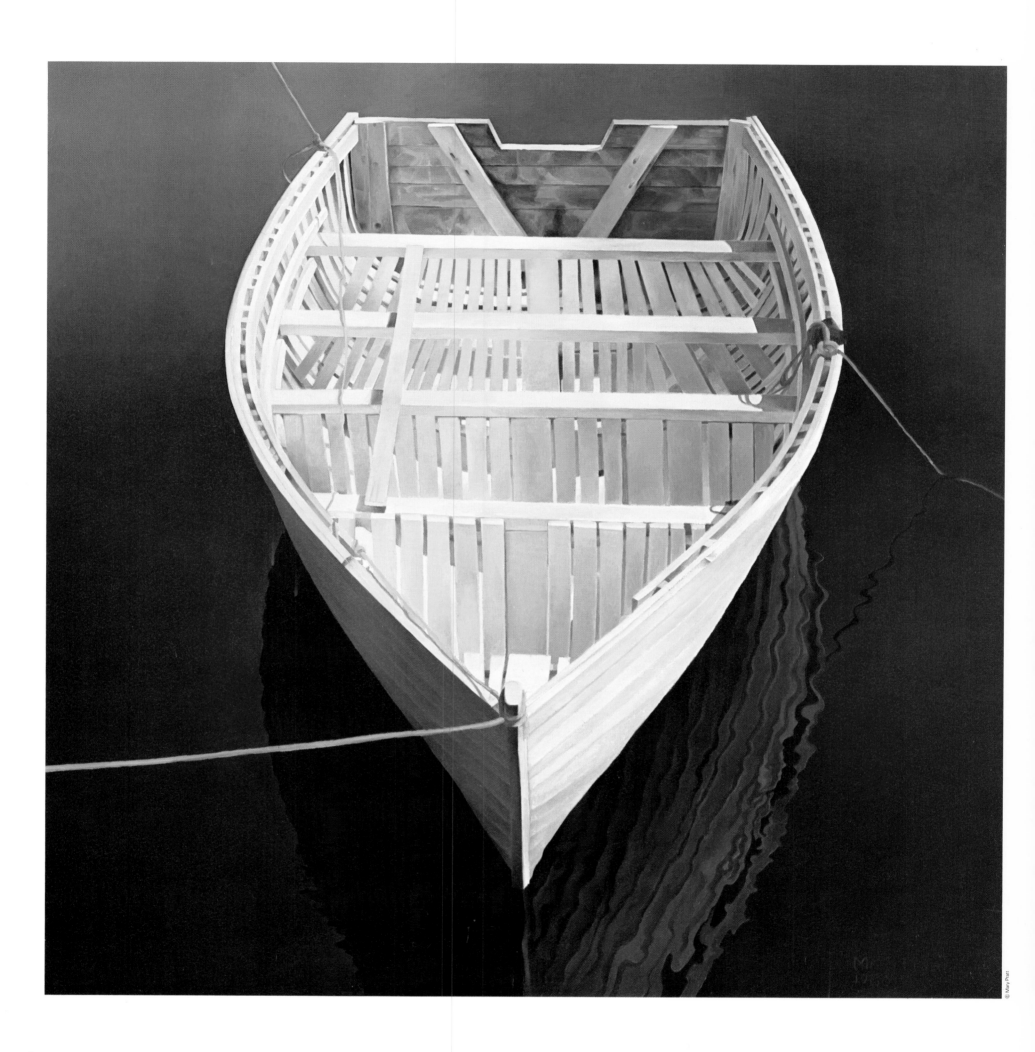

IMGAGES

2

Lionel Le Moine FitzGerald
"Still Life with Hat"
Oil on masonite, 61.0 cm x 71.0 cm, *c.* 1955
Private collection

IMAGES

3

Gerald Zeldin
''Lemon Glow''
Watercolour gouache, 30" x 40", 1978
Private collection

IMAGES
4

J. Fenwick Lansdowne
"Western Bluebird"
Watercolour on David Cox paper, 14" x 20", 1976
Courtesy of M. F. Feheley Arts Company Ltd., Toronto

J.F. LANSDOWNE
·1976·

IMAGES

5

D. P. Brown
"The Auction"
Egg tempera on panel, 34" x 48", 1975
Private collection

IMAGES
6

Ivan Eyre
"Pasture"
Acrylic on canvas, 56" x 64", 1979
Courtesy of the Polysar Limited Art Collection

IMAGES
7

Dulcie Foo Fat
"Cabbage"
Oil on canvas, 37" x 55", 1974
Collection: Visual Arts Branch, Government of Alberta, Edmonton

IMAGES

8

John Hall
"Sunset"
Acrylic on canvas, 44" x 44", 1979
Collection: Canada Council Art Bank

IMAGES
9

Jean Paul Lemieux
''Amélie et le temps''
Oil on canvas, 29" x 71", 1965
Courtesy of the Roberts Gallery, Toronto

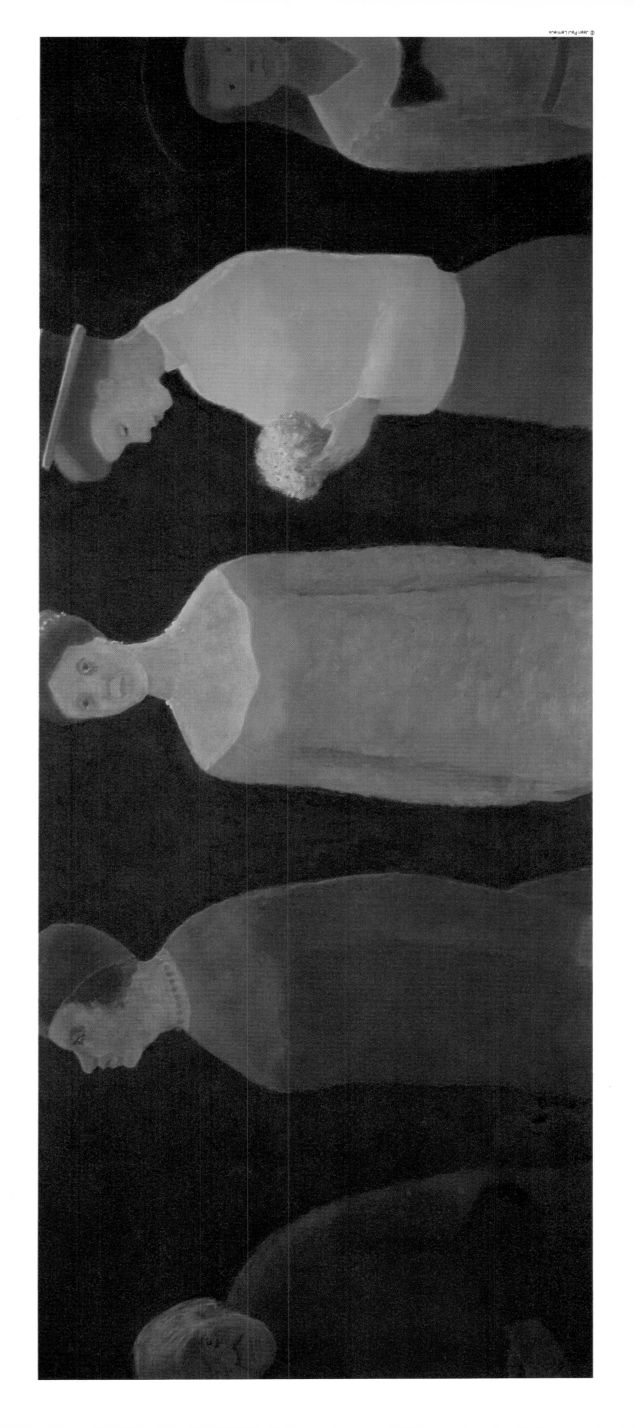

IMAGES
10

Tom Forrestall
"London Apartment"
Egg tempera on panel, 24¼" x 14", 1975
Courtesy of the artist

IMAGES
11

Ronald Stephen Mennie
"Late Lake Show"
Acrylic on board, 14" x 18½", 1980
Courtesy of the DeVooght Gallery, Vancouver
Collection: G. Bourgard, Edmonton

IMAGES

12

Ernest Lindner
"Skeleton of the Forest"
Watercolour, 75.2 cm x 55.5 cm, 1966
Collection: Winnipeg Art Gallery, Winnipeg
Acquired with the assistance of the Canada Council

E. Lindner 1966

IMAGES

13

Bruce St. Clair
''The Lord's Supper''
Oil on panel, 16″ x 22″, 1977
Courtesy of the Aggregation Gallery, Toronto
Private collection

B. St. Clair '77

IMAGES
14

E. J. Hughes
"Museum Ship (Penticton, B.C.)"
Oil on canvas, 25" x 30", 1959
Collection: Alumni Collection of the University of Western Ontario, London

E. J. Hughes

IMAGES
15

Richard Davis
"Cold Front"
Acrylic on board, 44" x 48", 1974-76
Courtesy of the Atelier Gallery, Vancouver
Private collection

IMAGES
16

Joseph Devellano
"Buck"
Egg tempera, 24" x 24", 1979
Courtesy of the Aggregation Gallery, Toronto
Private collection

IMAGES
17

Ken Danby
"Corner Window"
Watercolour, 21" x 27", 1973
Courtesy of Gallery Moos, Toronto
Private collection

IMAGES
18

James Spencer
"Mount Jacobsen #2"
Acrylic on canvas, 289.5 cm x 378.4 cm, 1974-75
Collection: Winnipeg Art Gallery, Winnipeg
Donated by the Women's Committee

IMAGES
19

Alex Colville
"Swimming Dog and Canoe"
Acrylic on particle board, 53 cm x 119 cm, 1979
Private collection, Geneva

IMAGES
20

Ken Suzana
"Dos Playas"
Acrylic on canvas, 87" x 58", 1979
Courtesy of the Aggregation Gallery, Toronto
Collection: Leland and Anne Verner

MARY PRATT was born in 1935 in Fredericton, New Brunswick. She studied at the University of New Brunswick Summer School under Fritz Banter and G. Pinsky, and at Mount Allison School of Fine Arts. As the mother of four children, she had little time to devote to her painting until 1965. She lives in St. Mary's Bay, Newfoundland.

LIONEL LE MOINE FITZ GERALD was born in 1890 in Winnipeg, Manitoba. He studied at A. S. Keszthelyi's School of Art in Winnipeg and, in 1921, attended the Art Students' League in New York, studying under Boardman Robinson and Kenneth Hayes Miller. In 1924 FitzGerald returned to Winnipeg to teach at the Winnipeg Art School, of which he became principal in 1928. Except for brief visits to Bowen Island near Vancouver and a visit to Mexico in 1951, he stayed in Winnipeg for most of his life. In 1932 he replaced J.E.H. MacDonald as one of the last members of the Group of Seven and in 1933 he was a founding member of the Canadian Group of Painters. He died in Snowflake, Manitoba, in 1956.

GERALD ZELDIN was born in Toronto, Ontario, in 1943. In 1965 he graduated from the Ontario College of Art and in 1967 obtained his Master of Fine Arts degree from the Claremont Graduate School in Claremont, California. He held teaching positions in 1971 at the Ontario College of Art, in 1972 at the University of Waterloo in the Department of Architecture, and in 1973 at the University of Toronto in the Department of Education. Since 1975 he has taught at the Dundas Valley School of Art. Zeldin lives in Dundas, Ontario.

J. FENWICK LANSDOWNE was born in 1937, in Hong Kong, of British parents. He moved to Canada in 1940 and was educated at St. Michael's School and Victoria High School in British Columbia. Lansdowne became interested in birds at the age of five and first attempted to paint them in 1950. From 1951 to 1952 he studied birds and their anatomy at the Provincial Museum in Victoria, B.C., where he first exhibited in 1952. Lansdowne received no formal instruction in art. In 1974 he became a member of the Royal Canadian Academy. He lives in Victoria, B.C.

D.P. BROWN was born in Forestville, Ontario, in 1939. As a child he travelled with his parents throughout Europe. He attended Clayesmore School at Iwerneminster in Dorset, England. In London, England, he met Lawren Harris who encouraged him to study art at Mount Allison University in Sackville, Nova Scotia. Brown enrolled at Mount Allison in 1958 and studied under

Lawren Harris, Alex Colville, and Edward Pulford before graduating with a Bachelor of Fine Arts degree in 1961. Upon graduation he moved to a farm near Aurora, Ontario. Between 1963 and 1968 he exhibited with the Banfer Gallery in New York. He lives in Collingwood.

IVAN EYRE was born in 1935 in Tully, Saskatchewan. Between 1950 and 1953 he studied under Ernest Lindner and in 1952 under Eli Nornstein. Eyre graduated with his Bachelor of Fine Arts degree from the University of Manitoba School of Art in 1957, was Graduate Assistant at the University of North Dakota in 1959, and for the next ten years was an instructor at the University of Manitoba School of Art. In 1966-67 he lived in Europe with the aid of a Canada Council grant. He currently lives in Winnipeg.

DULCIE FOO FAT was born in 1946 in England. In 1969 she received a B.A. (Honours) in Fine Art from Reading University and in 1970 received a Post-Graduate Teaching Certificate from Whitelands College, London. In 1974 she graduated from the University of Calgary with a Master of Fine Art degree. In 1977-78 she received a Canada Council grant. She lives in Calgary, Alberta.

JOHN HALL was born in Edmonton, Alberta, in 1943. He studied at the Alberta College of Art from 1960 to 1965 and at the Instituto Allende in Mexico in 1965-66. From 1969 to 1970 he was a visiting instructor in Fine Art at Ohio Wesleyan University, Delaware, Ohio, and he returned to Alberta in 1970 to teach at the Alberta College of Art in Calgary and at the University of Calgary in 1971. In 1975 Hall was elected to membership in the Royal Canadian Academy of Arts. Prior to returning to Calgary to live in 1980, he worked in New York.

JEAN PAUL LEMIEUX was born in Quebec City in 1904. He studied with the Brothers of the Christian Schools in California, returning to Montreal in 1917 to Loyola College. He subsequently attended the Ecole des Beaux Arts, Quebec, until 1934 — including a year of study in Paris in 1929. From 1937 to 1965 he taught at the Ecole des Beaux Arts. Today he lives and paints in Quebec City and Isles aux Coudres, Quebec.

TOM FORRESTALL was born in 1936 in the Annapolis Valley at Middleton, Nova Scotia. He moved with his family to Dartmouth where he attended children's art classes at the Nova Scotia School of Art. He was encouraged by his father in his desire to become a painter. Between 1954 and 1958 he studied at Mount Allison University under Alex Colville, Lawren Harris, and

Edmund Pulford. In 1958-59 he travelled and studied in Europe with the aid of a Canada Council grant, returning in 1959 to become the assistant curator of the Beaverbrook Art Gallery in Fredericton, New Brunswick. After 1960 he was able to devote all of his time to his painting and for the next thirteen years he remained in Fredericton. In 1972 he returned to Dartmouth where he now lives.

RONALD STEPHEN MENNIE was born in 1945 in Revelstoke, B.C. He attended the Ontario College of Art between 1963 and 1968 and the University of British Columbia between 1970 and 1971. He has worked as a commercial illustrator in Toronto and has received two awards of Merit from the Toronto-Montreal Art Directors Club for editorial illustration. He lives in Sorrento, B.C.

ERNEST LINDNER was born in 1897 in Vienna, Austria. In 1923 he joined the firm of Oswald Lindner there as a designer. He emigrated to Canada in 1926 and worked on a farm as a hired hand, settling in Saskatoon. Lindner spent the winter of 1926-27 at Luther College, Saskatoon, taking night classes in figure drawing from Gus Kenderdine. In 1931 he started teaching night classes in art at Saskatoon Technical Collegiate Institute, teaching full time from 1936 to 1962 and becoming Head of the Art Department from 1956 to 1960. Lindner has travelled extensively in Europe with the aid of a Canada Council grant and has studied etching and stone lithography in Vienna. He lives in Saskatoon.

BRUCE ST. CLAIR, born in 1945 in Galt, Ontario, studied at the Ontario College of Art between 1964 and 1967. He left OCA in 1967 to begin a program of independent study of painting. In 1967-68 he travelled extensively in Ontario, particularly in the Magnetawan River area. In 1969 he settled in the Lake Nipissing area in Northern Ontario where he still lives.

E. J. HUGHES, born in Vancouver in 1913, grew up in Nanaimo, on the east coast of Vancouver Island. At the age of sixteen he enrolled in the Vancouver School of Art where he studied for six years under Jock MacDonald and F. H. Varley. Upon graduation Hughes worked as a commercial artist in Vancouver with Paul Goranson and Orville Fisher. In 1939, he enlisted with the Royal Canadian Artillery; he was appointed to the position of Official War Artist in 1942. After his discharge in 1946, Hughes returned to Victoria and in 1951 moved thirty miles north to Shawnigan. He was discovered by Dr. Max Stern and had his first show at the Dominion Gallery in Montreal in 1954. Hughes still lives in Shawnigan.

RICHARD DAVIS, born in Middletown, New York, in 1947, entered the Pennsylvania Academy of Fine Arts in Philadelphia in 1965. In 1968 he came to Canada, becoming increasingly involved in fine art here until in 1972 he committed himself to work as a full-time painter and print-maker. Davis lives in Vancouver.

JOSEPH DEVELLANO was born in 1945 in Hamilton, Ontario. He studied at the Ontario College of Art from 1964 to 1967. Until recently he worked commercially but is now able to devote himself full time to his painting. Devellano lives in Dundas, Ontario.

KEN DANBY was born in Sault Ste. Marie, Ontario, in 1940. He studied under Jock MacDonald at the Ontario College of Art between 1957 and 1960 and then went on to work commercially in Toronto. In 1962, after attending a show of Andrew Wyeth's paintings at the Albright Knox Gallery in Buffalo, Danby decided to move away from abstract painting and back to realism. In 1964 he began painting full time and showing with Gallery Moos in Toronto. In 1966 he moved from Toronto to Rockwood, near Guelph, Ontario.

JAMES SPENCER was born in 1940 in Wolfville, Nova Scotia, where he attended Acadia University. He also attended the Ontario College of Art. Spencer has taught art at Central Technical School, Toronto; Mohawk College, Hamilton; Dundas Valley School of Art; McMaster University, Hamilton; and the Banff School of Fine Arts. He lives in Toronto.

ALEX COLVILLE was born in 1920 in Toronto, Ontario. In 1929 he moved with his family to Amherst, Nova Scotia, where he joined painting classes run by Mrs. Sarah S. Hart. At these classes Colville met Stanley Royle who recommended that he study at Mount Allison University. In 1942 Colville graduated from Mount Allison University with a Bachelor of Fine Arts degree. From 1944 to 1946 he was an Official War Artist in the Mediterranean and Northern Europe. He returned to Mount Allison in 1946 to teach painting, drawing, and art history. In 1963 he had a sell-out show at the Banfer Gallery in New York and decided to leave teaching; he has devoted himself to painting full time since then and lives in Sackville, Nova Scotia.

KEN SUZANA was born in 1948 in Windsor, Ontario. From 1967 to 1970 he studied at the School of Architecture at the University of Toronto. Suzana is a self-taught painter. He lives in Toronto.